The Romanovs

The
Romanovs
Family of Faith and Charity

Maria Maximova

Illustrated by Victoria Kitavina

Translated by Nicholas Kotar

HOLY TRINITY PUBLICATIONS

The Printshop of St Job of Pochaev
Holy Trinity Monastery
Jordanville, New York
2018

Printed with the blessing of His Eminence,
Metropolitan Hilarion,
First Hierarch of the Russian Orthodox Church
Outside of Russia

The Romanovs: Family of Faith and Charity
Text © 2018 Holy Trinity Monastery
Illustrations © 2017 Nikea Publishing House
Compilation © 2018 Holy Trinity Monastery

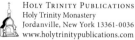

PSJP

PRINTSHOP OF
SAINT JOB OF POCHAEV

An imprint of

HOLY TRINITY PUBLICATIONS
Holy Trinity Monastery
Jordanville, New York 13361-0036
www.holytrinitypublications.com

ISBN: 978-0-88465-468-1 (hardback)

Library of Congress Control Number 2018936851

The Russian language edition was published
by the Nikea Publishing House in 2017, Moscow.
ISBN 978-5-91761-764-0

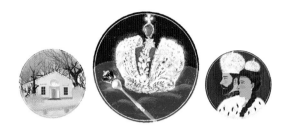

D O YOU KNOW THE HISTORY OF YOUR country? What about your family's history? Can you imagine how your great-grandmothers and great-grandfathers lived? What about your ancestors even farther back than that? No? Well, you should ask your relatives, maybe they'll tell you something. After all, each family has such interesting and important stories, and they might even help you in your life. And if these stories are not just tales of beautiful weddings and happy meetings, but memories of painful and terrifying events, don't be afraid! Every family's story is connected to the story of a country, and often it gives us examples of courage, endurance, wisdom, love, and faith.

Now you're going to hear a story about the last Russian emperor and his family. It's a story that people still talk and argue about today. People still write books about them and make movies about their life. Here's why.

When he was a boy, the future emperor Nicholas Romanov, together with his brothers and sisters, always dressed simply. They were athletic and even slept on uncomfortably hard beds. No one spoiled them with sweets or delicacies. They were raised to love work, to face difficulties bravely. They were prepared for a hard life.

Nicholas read a great deal, surprising his teachers with his excellent memory and unusual talents. He finished advanced courses in economics, law, and military studies. He even had practical military training in the infantry, cavalry, artillery, and the navy. And he was fluent in three languages.

He made sure to cement all his knowledge with practical training also. To do that, the future Tsar took part in an amazing naval journey. He was on a ship that almost circumnavigated the globe, visiting many countries—even Japan! From Japan to Russia, he traveled in carts and carriages throughout the Far East, Siberia, and the Ural Mountains. He encountered many dangers on the road. He even almost died a few times. But he came to know many different peoples and customs. He took part in official diplomatic missions that were very important for the Russian Empire. This

meant that when he became Tsar of Russia, he was one of the most educated people in all of Europe.

Nicholas Romanov met his future wife, Alix of Hesse-Darmstadt, at the wedding of his uncle the Grand Prince Sergei Alexandrovich. Alix came to Russia with her father for the wedding of her sister—Elizabeth Feodorovna (as she came to be known in Russia). Twelve-year-old Alix sat next to a young man at the triumphant wedding feast. This young man was the heir to the Russian throne, the Grand Prince Nicholas Alexandrovich Romanov.

After a few days, they took walks in the park together, talked about everything under the sun, laughed in each other's company… Suddenly, they realized that they were in love. In secret, they etched their names on the windowsill of the "Italian house" in

Nicholas Romanov took part in an amazing naval journey.

Peterhof Palace. That evening, Nicholas wrote in his diary; "We love each other." He gave her a present—a small brooch. At first, she accepted it, but then she decided that it was impossible to accept a gift, even from such a pleasant young man. After all, she didn't even know him that well. At a children's ball in the Anichkov Palace, as she danced with Nicholas, she slipped him a piece of paper. It held the brooch that he had given her. Nicholas was very upset, but her dignity only made him love Alix even more. This was the beginning of their wonderful romance.

Alix was herself born into a royal family. Her parents were Louis IV, Grand Duke of Hesse and by Rhine, and Princess Alice, the daughter of Queen Victoria of the United Kingdom. They believed that royal children needed to learn to work

hard, for only worthy people are capable of ruling countries.

Imagine this: every week, the children of this royal family would travel with their mother to different hospitals, orphanages, and rest homes for invalids. They would bring large bouquets of flowers, place them in vases and put them in the rooms of the sick. They helped the poor, the crippled, the old… And these people weren't even their relatives! Alix's parents were sure that this was the only way to raise her in the spirit of Christianity, to teach her not to consider herself better than others, to help others, to come to people's aid in difficult moments. The granddaughters of Queen Victoria definitely didn't grow up as lily-handed spoiled brats!

Of all Louis's children, Alix was the most serious and thoughtful. She didn't like to read the popular French novels of her time. Instead, she read "grown-up" essays about the history of religion and philosophy. She even wrote her own essays about those topics.

"I can't shine in society," she wrote, "because I don't have any grace or wittiness, both of which are so necessary for society. I love the spiritual content of life. This is what attracts me with such great power."

At the same time, she was so kind, sensitive, and gentle that her friends called her "our little sun."

The next time Alix came to Russia, she was seventeen. She spent a few weeks visiting her sister Elizabeth. This time, she met Nicholas often, and these meetings were a source of joy for them both. Now they

knew that they loved each other truly, that they could not live without each other.

After this, Nicholas finally told his parents about their love, insisting he wanted to marry the girl he loved so much. His parents didn't agree at first, but they couldn't refuse him. After all, their son was asking their permission to be happy! But they insisted on one condition. Alix had to become Orthodox.

Nicholas convinced Alix to become Orthodox. In that conversation, he said, "When you realize how beautiful, grace-filled, and humble is our Orthodox faith, how majestic our churches and monasteries, and how triumphant and stately our services, you will love them too. Then, nothing will divide us!"

Alix accepted Orthodoxy with her whole soul, deeply and sincerely. St John of Kronstadt was the one who performed the rite of acceptance into the Orthodox Church. Soon afterward, Nicholas and Alix were married. Alix became Alexandra Feodorovna, the empress of Russia.

Nicholas Romanov's father, Emperor Alexander III, told his son, "Strengthen your family, because the family is the foundation of every government."

Nicholas followed this advice his whole life. Alexandra Feodorovna was his best friend and faithful companion both in times of joy and in times of trouble. They lived in perfect harmony, adoring each other their whole lives, though hardly any married couple experiences as many difficulties as they did.

They had five children—Olga, Tatiana, Maria, Anastasia, and the heir to the throne, Alexei. The oldest daughter, Olga, was a true Russian beauty with a bright mind and a strong character. Tatiana was thoughtful, moderate, strict with herself, and level-headed. Maria was kind, easygoing, and cheerful. As she showed no arrogance, her siblings called her "Mashka" (a simple peasant's nickname). Anastasia was witty, high-spirited, mischievous, but well intentioned. Each was more beautiful and

pleasant than the next. They loved each other very much and even came up with their own common nickname—OTMA—an acronym of their first names.

The long-awaited son and heir, Alexei, was the family's favorite. He was smart, observant, sensitive, gentle, and joyful. Everything would have been wonderful, if not for his hemophilia, a disease where blood doesn't clot well. What that means is that normal boyish activities like riding a wooden horse or sledding or swinging on a swing set were dangerous for him. Whenever he played, his whole family watched, holding their breath with fear. When he couldn't sleep for nights on end from the pain, his sisters helped him as much as they could. They read to him, distracted him with stories, and played on the piano.

Alexei's sickness made him patient and gave him a strong will. With other people, he was easygoing and sincere, and he had a kind heart.

"When I become Tsar," he said, "there will be no more poor or suffering people. I want everyone to be happy."

His father taught him to respect the Russian soldier. He often took his son to official military inspections, even showing him the new flotilla of submarines in Riga one time. You can imagine what an impression they made on the little boy! Covered in ice in negative thirty-degree weather, they looked really imposing. This was far more interesting than any toys!

The Tsar and Tsaritsa believed that all people were equal in the eyes of God. No one should be proud of his position in the world. Therefore, they tried to live modestly, or as much as their exalted position allowed them. Nicholas preferred to eat simple porridge and cabbage soup, instead of the fancy meals offered in the palace. He had no problem bathing in the lake together with other men.

In the evening, he often sat together with the family, reading to them.

The royal children were raised in simplicity and strictness. Even the girls slept on rough cots without pillows, two of them per room. They dressed modestly, and the younger children wore their older siblings' hand-me-downs. The parents insisted that their children had to learn how to deny their own wishes for the sake of others. The Tsar loved to say, "The more important a person, the faster should he help everyone and never remind anyone of his greatness. This is how my children must be also."

The royal family also loved sports. One time, they all kayaked over two and a half miles along the Finnish coastline through an archipelago of rocky islands that were divided only by narrow straits. Nicholas II had a passion for kayaks since his childhood, ever since his parents gave him his first kayak on his thirteenth birthday.

Of course, this was also a truly Orthodox family. The Tsaritsa and her daughters loved to sing in church during the Divine Liturgy. "For God, nothing is impossible," the Tsaritsa wrote, "I believe … that whoever is pure in soul will always be heard. To such a person, no difficulty or danger in life is frightening, since they are only insurmountable to those people who have a shallow or insufficient faith."

It seemed that this family was created for joy, to live quietly as a happy family. In her journal, the Empress Alexandra wrote, "Love needs its daily bread." She meant that daily happiness is made up of individual moments, a heartfelt look, a smile, a kind word, a helping hand extended at the right moment. However, it wouldn't be wrong to

say that the Tsar had the most dangerous
and thankless job in the world.

The twentieth century overwhelmed Russia with wars and troubles. And then, lightning struck. World War I began.

Nicholas II traveled to the mission of the monastery of Diveyevo in St Petersburg to seek consolation. He prayed for a very long time about Russia before the icon of St Seraphim of Sarov. He wept. With his whole heart, he believed in God's providence. He believed that not a single hair can fall from the head of a person if God didn't will it.

Alexandra Feodorovna finished a course of study in nursing during the war. Together with her daughters, she tended to the wounded from morning until night in the military hospitals. She was the first Tsaritsa in the history of Russia to be a nurse! Alexandra Feodorovna worked in the operating room, helping the surgeons during the most difficult surgeries. She worked with quiet humility and tirelessness, as though it were her destiny to work as a nurse. During especially painful surgeries, soldiers would often beg the Tsaritsa to be near them. She comforted the wounded and prayed together with them.

Princess Olga took it upon herself to hand out the morning medicine to all the wounded. She did this with unusual dedication. Tatiana bandaged wounds and

helped the surgeons in the operating room. She was tidy, careful, and good at her work.

As for Tsarevich Alexei, he traveled with his father to the front. Even though he was only 10 to 11 years old, he had firsthand experience of bombing, and he truly knew what war was, not only from reading books.

In the winter of 1917, riots broke out in Petrograd (the name given to St Petersburg when the war with Germany began in 1914).

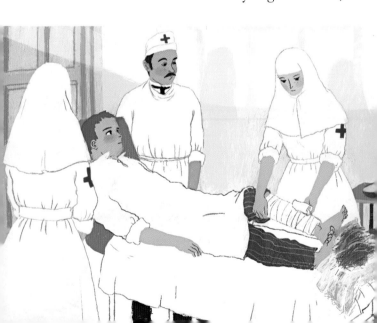

The people were sick of the war, and rumors flew about that trains carrying bread for the capital had been delayed, and that famine was coming. Soldiers began to break their vows of loyalty, switching to the side of the rioters. People started looting, workers stopped working, and mass demonstrations against the government and the Tsar broke out.

And then, the fateful day came. Nicholas II signed a manifesto of abdication from the throne. With pain in his heart, he made this decision, bombarded on all sides by demands from his military commanders and closest advisers, who insisted that this was necessary to save Russia.

"If I am an obstacle to Russia's well-being, and everyone in positions of authority is begging me to abdicate the throne, I am ready to do this. I am ready not only to

abandon my kingdom, but even my life, for the sake of my homeland." This is what the Tsar thought to himself.

He was upset and lonely. He was also worried about this family. They were alone in Tsarskoye Selo, the children were sick, and no one seemed willing to defend them…

The Provisional Government came to power and decided to arrest the royal family. Looters and rioters overwhelmed Tsarskoye Selo. Something unheard-of was happening in the streets—drunk soldiers, some with rifles, some without, ran back and forth, grabbing everything they could carry from the stores. Part of the army rioted, and a huge crowd of more than ten thousand people began to march toward the royal palace.

You can imagine what the helpless mother of five seriously ill children felt! In this difficult hour, she decided to pray before the miracle-working icon of the Mother of God of the Sign. With tears in her eyes, on her knees, the earthly queen fervently begged the Queen of Heaven for help and intercession. By this time, rioting soldiers surrounded the palace.

General Kornilov walked into the room of the Tsaritsa.

"Your Imperial Highness," he said, "You must not be aware of what's happening in Petrograd and Tsarskoye Selo. It is very unpleasant and difficult for me to tell you this, but for the sake of your safety, I must…" He stopped in confusion.

She held back her fear and anger, never losing her calmness of spirit, holding herself strictly in check.

"I know all this," she said. "Have you come to arrest me?"

"Yes, exactly," answered Kornilov.

"And what does that mean for us?"

"You will be deprived of your royal guard. Instead, you will have a common guard of garrisoned soldiers. You are forbidden from using the telephone, and all your letters will be censored."

"Nothing else?"

"Nothing else."

Saying not another word, Alexandra Feodorovna turned and walked away from him.

People began to spread vile rumors about the Romanovs collaborating with the enemy, as though they were German spies. It is difficult to think of a more idiotic lie. However, during the days of the war, everyone was searching for "German spies." People were sick of the war, and even the term "German" had become a curse word. And who was Alexandra Feodorovna by birth? A German, after all!

The royal family was subjected to constant searches and interrogations. But no one ever found a shred of evidence to prove they were traitors. When a member of the commission of inquiry asked why the royal family's correspondence was not yet made public, he was told, "If we make it public, the people will begin revering them as saints!"

Even while under arrest in Tsarskoye Selo, the Romanovs tried not to become depressed. In the winter, the Tsar and his children shoveled snow together. In the spring, they chopped down trees. In the summer, they worked in the garden. The tirelessness of the Tsar so amazed the soldiers that one of them said, "If you give him a piece of land to work on, soon he will win for himself the whole of the Russian land again."

The life of the prisoners was filled with humiliating difficulties. The Tsar was not allowed to live together with his wife, only seeing her when they sat together for meals. Their guards made crude remarks. No family members were allowed to visit the royal family. One time, a soldier even took away

Alexei's toy rifle, saying that he was not allowed to bear arms.

Soon, the Provincial Government ordered that the royal prisoners be moved to Tobolsk in Siberia. They claimed it was to protect them from possible dangers.

And so, for the last time, the royal family walked through their favorite park with its so-called children's island. They visited their garden for the last time, then turned to see the dark windows of their palace... This was their home, and they left it with a feeling of sorrow and bitterness.

Nicholas Alexandrovich Romanov had already been in Tobolsk. He recognized the white kremlin, the cathedral, the churches built on hills. When he, as the young heir to the throne, returned from his journey through Europe and Asia, he stopped in this old Siberian city. He liked it very much.

But now, the royal family was basically in exile. None of them were allowed to even leave the house without permission. They could not take walks in the city.

The children, together with their parents, endured all their privations with meekness and humility. But they were young, and they wanted to live, to rejoice in the sun, to laugh, to play, to investigate the world! And so, they continued to study, they put on plays in French, English, and Russian. But never, not even in passing, did they complain.

They tried not to let fear or despair enter their souls.

The princesses built for themselves a sledding hill in winter. Everyone sledded down the hill, from Alexei to the Tsar and Tsaritsa. When they prepared for Christmas, each of them made presents for each other with their own hands. They even

made presents for their guards. After all,
the feast was for everyone! The Provincial
Government had to keep changing the
guards, because the soldiers—seeing the
kindness, meekness, and love of the family
for each other—were filled with respect for
the royal family.

Their house had a small garden, and
their cook built an enclosure for fowl. The
princesses spent much of their time there,
taking care of the chickens and ducks. They
also planted their own vegetables—carrots,
potatoes, and beets.

The Tsar loved physical work, and he
spent most of his time sawing round timber
for the winter. His daughters tried to keep
up with him. They also chopped, sawed, and
piled wood, and they did all this with joy,
singing and encouraging each other.

In the meantime, the Revolution happened, and the Bolsheviks came to power in Petrograd. And thus began the period that the Tsar described in his diary with these words: "These events are much worse and more shameful even than the Time of Troubles." The Romanovs were no longer allowed to attend church. They barely managed to get permission to attend services on the twelve major feasts. The family was now given soldiers' rations. In the meantime, in Tobolsk itself, soldiers of the Red Army were disarming former officers, and many supporters of the former regime were simply shot.

One time, a soldier walked into the Tsar's room with his rifle cocked and said, smirking, "We just ordered all the officers to take off their epaulets, and Tsar Nikolashka has to do

the same." He was ready to rudely rip off the
Emperor's epaulets then and there.

Nicholas turned aside carefully and forcefully asked, "What other orders do you have?"

"You have to be photographed in profile and in full face. Like prisoners. Just as you did to us, now we're going to do to you. It's a new government now. Lenin and the Bolsheviks have taken over."

Soon the commissar of the new Bolshevik government came to the Tsar and

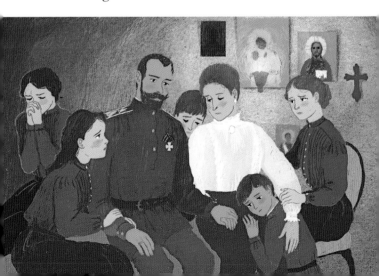

announced, "I have to take your family away from here. But since Alexei Nikolaevich is sick, I will only take you."

"I will not go anywhere," said the Tsar.

"I strongly recommend that you listen to me. Otherwise I may have to use force or resign my post. In that case, another man will come, and he will not be as kind as I am. You must be ready by four o'clock tomorrow."

They decided that three of them would go—Nicholas, Alexandra, and Maria. The rest remained in Tobolsk and joined them later.

It was early spring. The road was difficult; there were mudslides. In the morning, carriages were prepared. Although you could hardly call them carriages. They were simple Siberian "koshevy"—deep and wide sleds with a high back, lined with felt matting. It was a peasant's form of transportation. And

so, the royal family began their final journey
to Ekaterinburg.

In Ekaterinburg, it immediately became obvious that they were no longer in exile. They were practically in jail. Here, the former emperor was called "citizen Romanov" for the first time, and no one was allowed to address him as "Your Highness."

They were all searched, and all their best things were simply taken away from them. Then, they were put under house arrest. They were only allowed to take short walks in the tiny prison-like yard. For the first time in their life, they were forbidden from attending the Paschal service. Only from a distance could they hear the ringing of Paschal bells.

Every day was a new torture. Their guards made themselves at home in the royal family's house, and at any moment, they could burst into the room. The guards watched their every move, listened in on every conversation. The princesses' rooms

didn't even have doors. The windows were painted over with white paint, so that sunlight couldn't get through into the dark and dim house. The prisoners couldn't even see the sky.

Even so, the royal family began each day with common prayer. Then the commandant would conduct a roll call, and only after this would the prisoners have the right to go about their business.

The young princesses, so modestly and nobly brought up, were not allowed to go to the bathroom without supervision. Every time they were led to the bathroom, the soldiers would pepper them with crude jokes. The soldiers sang crude songs in their presence and swore at them.

During lunch, the family of seven was only given five spoons. The guards sat with them at the table, smoking cigarettes and blowing the smoke into the children's faces…

One time, one of the guards even climbed up on the fence immediately outside the girls' bedrooms and began to sing inappropriate songs. Another time, when Anastasia looked out her window, a guard shot at her from his rifle. The bullet whizzed past her and landed in a lintel.

In spite of their fear of the guards, the girls found various useful and pleasant work to do. They never allowed themselves to be idle: they drew, embroidered, mended and washed their clothes. In the evenings, they kneaded flour, and in the mornings, they baked bread no worse than their cook.

They often sang together, especially spiritual songs. Often you could hear drunk, foul voices coming from the first floor, while at the same time, the rooms of the royal family on the second floor were filled with the heavenly sound of the Cherubic Hymn or other spiritual songs.

Alexei's serious and incurable illness paralyzed his legs, and so whenever the family took a walk, the Tsar carried him in his arms. He would put him carefully into a wheelchair and push him among the trees. The Tsarevich played with his dog Joy and with the cook's assistant Leonid Sednev, who was almost the same age as he. Leonid had served the Tsar's family while still in Tsarskoye Selo, and he accompanied them into exile. He was Grand Prince Alexei's last friend.

When you read how cruelly the royal family was treated in Siberia, you can't help but be amazed—how did they, especially the children, manage to endure it all? How could they have preserved their purity of heart? Why did they not hate their torturers? How could they have borne the curses of the soldiers, the foul language, and the drunken songs?

If you think about it, you'll understand that they endured everything because they were together, because they were a family. They supported each other, encouraged and

helped each other, trying never to despair. And because they believed in God.

Alexandra Feodorovna wrote from her exile: "You can endure anything if you feel God's presence and love and if you believe in Him at all times… You have to be grateful to God eternally for everything that He gave. And if He took it away, then maybe, if you don't complain about it, you will find even greater joy. You have to always hope. The Lord is so great, and you have to pray, constantly asking Him to save our dear Motherland… Even though it's dark now, the sun still shines in nature, giving us hope for something good in the future. You see, we haven't lost our faith, and I hope we'll never lose it. Only faith gives us strength, firmness of spirit to overcome everything. And we have to thank God for everything … Isn't that true? For now,

we and our dear little close-knit family
are alive."

The prisoners tried to live according to
the truth of the Gospel. They led a truly
pious and humble life. Faith gave them the
courage not only to endure their pain, but
even to forgive their tormentors. But how
hard it is to forgive our enemies! Still, the
royal daughters, who had so many good
reasons to be upset, were never angry at their
guards. Even the thought of judging them or
hating them or taking revenge on them was
far from their minds.

Later, a poem was found in the letters of
Olga Nikolaevna Romanova. It ended with
these lines:

At the threshold of the tomb
Breathe into the mouths of Your slaves

Your superhuman strength
To meekly pray for our enemies.

The children and the parents shared the difficulties of imprisonment equally. They felt that their death must be near. And so they lived, treasuring every day, every kind word, every moment of joyful companionship with their dear ones.

In imprisonment, the Tsar wrote, "Don't lose faith in God's mercy. He will not abandon the Motherland to perish. We have to endure all these humiliations, this filth, these horrors with submissiveness (since we don't have the power to help). And He will save, He Who is long-suffering and plenteous in mercy. He will not be angry with us until the end… Without faith, it would have been impossible to live."

Olga Nikolaevna wrote a letter from exile: "Father asks me to pass on to all who remain faithful to him not to avenge for his sake, since he has forgiven all and prays for all. Please do not seek vengeance for yourselves, but remember that the evil that is in the world now will be even stronger, and that it is not evil which conquers evil, but only love."

These are the words of a true Christian. This is true forgiveness of enemies!

Finally, their last hour came. On July 17, 1918, the whole royal family was killed in the basement of the Ipatiev House in Ekaterinburg, where they were living in exile. Together with the royal family, their servants

were shot as well, though they had followed them willingly into exile. These included Dr Eugene Bodkin, the cook Ivan Kharitonov, the Tsar's valet Alexei Trupp, and the maid Anna Demidova. The only one to survive was Grand Prince Alexei's friend Leonid, the cook's assistant.

In 1981, the Russian Orthodox Church Outside Russia canonized the royal family as part of the synaxis of the New Martyrs and Confessors of Russia. In 2000, the Synod of Bishops of the Russian Orthodox Church (Moscow Patriarchate) followed suit.

And now abideth faith, hope, charity, these three; but the greatest of these is charity.

1 Corinthians 13:13–KJV